REFLECTIONS ON
THE CRUCIFIXION
A Service of Tenebrae

Kathryn W. Orso

REFLECTIONS ON THE CRUCIFIXION

Scripture quotations, unless otherwise noted, are from THE LIVING BIBLE and are used with the permission of Tyndale House Publishers, Wheaton, Illinois.

REFLECTIONS ON THE CRUCIFIXION was originally published as a portion of the book, AS WE LOVE AND FORGIVE: RESOURCES FOR THE LENTEN SEASON, by Kathryn W. Orso, © MCMLXXV by the C.S.S. Publishing Company, Inc., Lima, Ohio.

Reprinted March 1989

978-0-89536-200-1   PRINTED IN U.S.A.

REFLECTIONS ON THE CRUCIFIXION
A Tenebrae Service

A meaningful service to use during the Lenten season is the "tenebrae" service. Tenebrae is the Latin word for "shadows." The tenebrae tradition commemorates Christ's suffering and death in a service that progresses from light to darkness. Many churches offer this special service on Good Friday, helping worshipers become aware of the agony of the Cross.

Setting for the Service

In a tenebrae service, the lights in the sanctuary are gradually dimmed. The service begins in light and ends in darkness.

To add to the effectiveness of the service, a seven-candle stick candelabrum can be used. As the service begins, all seven candles are lighted. As the service progresses, an acolyte extinguishes each candle at a specified time, until all candles are out.

In a church with an altar, two candelabra can be used, one being on each side of the Cross. A candle in each candelabrum is extinguished as the service indicates. If two acolytes are used, each one is responsible for extinguishing the candles on one of the candelabra.

Complete silence should be observed during the extinguishing of each candle.

Time of the Service

This service is designed to be used for either a one-hour or a three-hour worship experience. Some churches offer a three-hour service on Good Friday afternoon from noon to three p.m., the hours when Jesus was hanging on the Cross. Other churches have a one-hour service, either Good Friday afternoon or Good Friday evening.

The nature of the service also makes it possible to use various parts as brief devotions at midweek Lenten services.

The title sections printed in bold type are those to use in a one-hour service. The entire service, including the "bold" sections, will take approximately three hours.

Meditations in the Service

Suggested meditations for the Tenebrae Service can be found in "As We Love and Forgive," available from the C.S.S. Publishing Company. For either the one-hour or the three-hour service, reflections of the twelve disciples may be used.

Participants in the Service

Although the pastor alone can present the Tenebrae Service, it would be effective to have a number of other participants. The reflections of each of the twelve disciples could be presented by twelve different persons. It would add to the service if the "disciples" wore choir robes and were seated together in the front pew of the church. When each speaks, he should turn and face the congregation.

For the three-hour service, the participation of soloists and/or a choir is suggested. Although certain selections have been suggested, substitutions can be made if the theme of the service is followed.

Bulletins for the Congregation

Bulletins are available from the C.S.S. Publishing Company for the one-hour Tenebrae Service. The service will be more effective if each worshiper has a bulletin to follow. No announcements will have to be made if bulletins are used. The bulletins contain the words of the hymns, so that hymnals will not be needed.

(For a one-hour service, use only the sections titled in bold. For a three-hour service, use the entire printed service. For a three-hour service, note the places * where the worshipers may leave, if need be.)

Prelude, with Silent Meditation

Opening Hymn [Processional]
"In the Cross of Christ I Glory"

Call to Worship
Come to the Cross of Jesus.
Come and take your stand.
Come to the Cross of Jesus.
Come, join the faithful band. Amen.

Litany (During the litany, play the tune to "Beneath the Cross of Jesus" very softly.)
Pastor: Our hearts are heavy, as we worship our crucified Lord.
People: He lived for our sins.
Pastor: We watch with horror as we see him hanging on the Cross.
People: He died for our sins.
Pastor: We see the evil in the world around him.
People: He died for our sins.
Pastor: We, too, have denied our Lord.
People: He died for our sins.
Pastor: We, too, have betrayed our Lord.
People: He died for our sins.
All: Forgive us, Lord, and love us. Amen.

Hymn — "Beneath the Cross of Jesus"

Scripture Reading — Isaiah 52:13-53:12
See, my Servant shall prosper; he shall be highly exalted. Yet many shall be amazed when they see him — yes, even far-off foreign nations and their kings; they shall stand dumbfounded, speechless in his presence. For they shall see and understand what

they had not been told before. They shall see my Servant beaten and bloodied, so disfigured one would scarcely know it was a person standing there. So shall he cleanse many nations.

But, oh, how few believe it! Who will listen? To whom will God reveal his saving power? In God's eyes he was like a tender green shoot, sprouting from a root in dry and sterile ground. But in our eyes there was no attractiveness at all, nothing to make us want him. We despised him and rejected him — a man of sorrows, acquainted with bitterest grief. We turned our backs on him and looked the other way when he went by. He was despised and we didn't care.

Yet, it was our grief he bore, our sorrows that weighed him down. And we thought his troubles were a punishment from God, for his own sins! But he was wounded and bruised for our sins. He was chastised that we might have peace; he was lashed — and we were healed! We are the ones who strayed away like sheep! We, who left God's paths to follow our own. Yet God laid on him the guilt and sins of every one of us!

He was oppressed and he was afflicted, yet he never said a word. He was brought as a lamb to the slaughter; and as a sheep before her shearers is dumb, so he stood silent before the ones condemning him. From prison and trial they led him away to his death. But who among the people of that day realized it was their sins that he was dying for — that he was suffering their punishment? He was buried like a criminal in a rich man's grave; but he had done no wrong, and had never spoken an evil word.

Yet, it was the Lord's good plan to bruise him and fill him with grief. But when his soul had been made an offering for sin, then he shall have a multitude of children, many heirs. And when he sees all that is accomplished by the anguish of his soul, he shall be satisfied; and because of what he has experienced, my righteous Servant shall make many to be counted righteous before God, for he shall bear all their sins.

Therefore, I will give him the honors of one who is mighty and great, because he has poured out his soul unto death. He was counted as a sinner, and he bore the sins of many, and he pled with God for sinners.

Pastor: Jesus said, "Father, forgive them; for they know not what they do."

Anthem or Solo — "The Words on the Cross," Part I
           (Litany, 777,6, or Swedish litany, 77,76)
Jesus, in thy dying woes,
Even while thy lifeblood flows
Craving pardon for thy foes.
   Hear us, holy Jesus.

Savior, for our pardon sue,
When our sins thy pangs renew,
For we know not what we do:
   Hear us, holy Jesus.

O may we, who mercy need,
Be like thee in heart and deed,
When with wrong our spirits bleed:
   Hear us, holy Jesus. Amen.

Reflections of Andrew

Hymn — "There Is a Green Hill Far Away," vss. 1 and 2

Psalm 139 — Read responsively
O Lord, you have examined my heart and know everything about me:
   You know when I sit or stand. When far away you know my every thought.
You chart the path ahead of me, and tell me where to stop and rest. Every moment, you know where I am.
   You know what I am going to say before I even say it.

You both precede and follow me, and place your hand of blessing on my head.

This is too glorious, too wonderful to believe! I can never be lost to your Spirit! I can never get away from my God!

If I go up to heaven, you are there; if I go down to the place of the dead, you are there. If I ride the morning winds to the farthest oceans, even there your hand will guide me, your strength will support me.

If I try to hide in the darkness, the night becomes light around me. For even darkness cannot hide from God; to you the night shines as bright as day. Darkness and light are both alike to you.

You made all the delicate, inner parts of my body, and knit them together in my mother's womb. Thank you for making me so wonderfully complex! It is amazing to think about. Your workmanship is marvelous — and how well I know it.

You were there while I was being formed in utter seclusion! You saw me before I was born and scheduled every day of my life before I began to breathe. Every day was recorded in your Book!

How precious it is, Lord, to realize that you are thinking about me constantly! I can't even count how many times a day your thoughts turn toward me. And when I waken in the morning, you are still thinking of me!

Surely you will slay the wicked, Lord! Away, blood-thirsty men! Begone! They blaspheme your name and stand in arrogance against you — how silly can they be?

O Lord, shouldn't I hate those who hate you? Shouldn't I be grieved with them?

Yes, I hate them, for your enemies are my enemies, too.

All: Search me, O God, and know my heart; test my thoughts. Point out anything you find in me that makes you sad, and lead me along the path of everlasting life.

Reflections of Bartholomew

Hymn — "There Is a Green Hill Far Away," vss. 3 and 4

Extinguishing of First Candle — Silent meditation

* Quiet meditation, with soft music

Hymn — "The Old Rugged Cross"

Reflections of James, the Elder

Scripture — Matthew 27:22-37
"Then what shall I do with Jesus, your Messiah?" Pilate asked.

And they shouted, "Crucify him!"

"Why?" Pilate demanded. "What has he done wrong?" But they kept shouting, "Crucify him! Crucify!"

When Pilate saw that he wasn't getting anywhere, and that a riot was developing, he sent for a bowl of water and washed his hands before the crowd, saying, "I am innocent of the blood of this good man. The responsibility is yours!"

And the mob yelled back, "His blood be on us and on our children!"

Then Pilate released Barabbas to them. And after he had whipped Jesus, he gave him to the Roman soldiers to take away and crucify. But first they took him into the armory and called out the entire contingent. They stripped him and put a scarlet robe on him, and made a crown from long thorns and put it on his head, and placed a stick in his right hand as a scepter and knelt before him in mockery.

"Hail, King of the Jews," they yelled. And they spat on him and grabbed the stick and beat him on the head with it.

After the mockery, they took off the robe and put his own garment on him again, and took him out to crucify him. As they were on the way to the execution grounds they came across a man from Cyrene, in Africa — Simon was his name — and forced him to carry Jesus' cross. Then they went to an area known as Golgotha, that is, "Skull Hill," where the soldiers gave him drugged wine to drink; but when he had tasted it, he refused.

After the crucifixion, the soldiers threw dice to divide up his clothes among themselves. Then they sat around and watched him as he hung there. And they put a sign above his head, "This is Jesus, the King of the Jews."

Pastor: Jesus said, "Today shalt thou be with me in paradise."

Anthem or Solo — "The Words on the Cross," Part II
Jesus, pitying the sighs
Of the thief, who near thee dies,
Promising him paradise:
    Hear us, holy Jesus.

May we in our guilt and shame
Still thy love and mercy claim
Calling humbly on thy Name:
    Hear us, holy Jesus.

May our hearts to thee incline,
Looking from our cross to thine;
Cheer our souls with hope divine:
    Hear us, holy Jesus.

Prayer — In unison
Lord, forgive us for hiding often in the shadows, for failing to witness, and for questioning your

way. Guide us in a stronger loyalty, a firmer faith, and a steadfast hope. Amen.

Psalm 51:1-17 — Read antiphonally

Men: O Loving and kind God, have mercy. Have pity upon me and take away the awful stain of my transgressions.

Women: Oh, wash me, cleanse me, from this guilt. Let me be pure again.

Men: For I admit my shameful deed — it haunts me day and night.

Women: It is against you and you alone I sinned, and did this terrible thing. You saw it all, and your sentence against me is just.

Men: But I was born a sinner, yes, from the moment my mother conceived me.

Women: You deserve honesty from the heart; yes, utter sincerity and truthfulness. Oh, give me this wisdom.

Men: Sprinkle me with the cleansing blood and I shall be clean again. Wash me and I shall be whiter than snow.

Women: And after you have punished me, give me back my joy again.

Men: Don't keep looking at my sins — erase them from your sight.

All: Create in me a new, clean heart, O God, filled with clean thoughts and right desires. Don't toss me aside, banished forever from your presence. Don't take your Holy Spirit from me. Restore to me again the joy of your salvation, and make me willing to obey you. Then I will teach your ways to other sinners, and they — guilty like me — will repent and return to you.

Women: Don't sentence me to death. O, my God, you alone can rescue me. Then I will sing

of your forgiveness, for my lips will be unsealed — oh, how I will praise you.

All: You don't want penance; if you did, how gladly I would do it! You aren't interested in offerings burned before you on the altar. It is a broken spirit you want — remorse and penitence. A broken and a contrite heart, O God, you will not ignore.

Reflections of James, the Less

Hymn — "Alas, and Did My Saviour Bleed"

Extinguishing of Second Candle — Silent meditation

* Quiet meditation, with soft music

Hymn — "O Sacred Head, Now Wounded"

Reflections of John

Psalm 40:1-10 — Read responsively
I waited patiently for God to help me; then he listened and heard my cry.
He lifted me out of the pit of despair, out from the bog and the mire and set my feet on a hard, firm path and steadied me as I walked along.
He has given me a new song to sing, of praises to our God. Now many will hear of the glorious things he did for me, and stand in awe before the Lord, and put their trust in him.
Many blessings are given to those who trust the Lord, and have no confidence in those who are proud, or who trust in idols.
O, Lord, my God, many and many a time you have done great miracles for us and we are ever in your thoughts. Who else can do such glorious things? No one else can be compared with you. There isn't time to tell of all your wonderful deeds.
It isn't sacrifices and offerings which you really

want from your people. Burnt animals bring no special joy to your heart. But you have accepted the offer of my lifelong service.

Then I said, "See, I have come, just as all the prophets foretold.

And I delight to do your will, my God, for your law is written upon my heart!

I have told everyone the Good News that you forgive men's sins. I have not been timid about it, as you well know, O Lord.

I have not kept this Good News hidden in my heart, but have proclaimed your lovingkindness and truth to all the congregations."

Anthem or Solo — "The Words on the Cross," Part III

Jesus, loving to the end
Her whose heart thy sorrows rend,
And thy dearest human friend:
    Hear us, holy Jesus.

May we in thy sorrows share,
For thy sake all peril dare,
And enjoy thy tender care:
    Hear us, holy Jesus.

May we all thy loved ones be,
All one holy family,
Loving for the love of thee:
    Hear us, holy Jesus. Amen.

Pastor: And Jesus said, "Woman, behold thy son!"
        "Behold thy mother."

Litany

Pastor: Our minds cannot really comprehend the meaning of it all.

People: Hear us, holy Jesus.

Pastor: Our ears are deafened by what we hear.

People: Hear us, holy Jesus.

Pastor: Our eyes are blinded by what we see.

People: **Hear us, holy Jesus.**
Pastor: Our hearts are overwhelmed by what
we feel.
All: Come into our lives, Lord Jesus;
Come in today; come in to stay;
Come into our lives, Lord Jesus.

Scripture — Matthew 27:38-54

Two robbers were also crucified there that morning, one on either side of him. And the people passing by hurled abuse, shaking their heads at him and saying, "So! You can destroy the temple and build it again in three days, can you? Well, then, come on down from the cross if you are the Son of God!"

And the chief priests and Jewish leaders also mocked him. "He saved others," they scoffed, "but he can't save himself! So you are the King of Israel, are you? Come down from the cross and we'll believe you! He trusted God — let God show his approval by delivering him! Didn't he say, 'I am God's Son'?"

And the robbers also threw the same in his teeth.

That afternoon, the whole earth was covered with darkness for three hours, from noon until three o'clock.

About three o'clock, Jesus shouted, "Eli, Eli, lama sabachthani," which means, "My God, my God, why have you forsaken me?"

Some of the bystanders misunderstood and thought he was calling for Elijah. One of them ran and filled a sponge with sour wine and put it on a stick and held it up to him to drink. But the rest said, "Leave him alone. Let's see whether Elijah will come and save him."

Then Jesus shouted out again, dismissed his spirit, and died. And look! The curtain secluding the Holiest Place in the temple was split apart from top to bottom; and the earth shook, and rocks broke, and tombs opened, and many godly men and women who had died came back to life again. After Jesus' resurrection, they left the cemetery and went into Jerusalem, and appeared to many people there.

The soldiers at the crucifixion and their sergeant were terribly frightened by the earthquake and all that happened. They exclaimed, "Surely, this was God's Son."

Reflections of Judas

Hymn — "When I Survey the Wondrous Cross"

Extinguishing of Third Candle — Silent meditation

* Quiet meditation, with soft music

Hymn — "Ah, Holy Jesus"

Reflections of Jude

Psalm 22:1-5; 9-11 — Read responsively
My God, my God, why have you forsaken me? Why do you refuse to help me or even to listen to my groans?
Day and night, I keep on weeping, crying for your help, but there is no reply — for you are holy.
The praises of our fathers surrounded your throne; they trusted you and you delivered them.
You heard their cries for help and saved them; they were never disappointed when they sought your aid.
Lord, how you have helped me before! You took me safely from my mother's womb and brought me through the years of infancy.
I have depended upon you since birth; you have always been my God. Don't leave me now, for trouble is near and no one else can possibly help.

Pastor: Jesus cried, "My God, my God, why have you forsaken me?"

16

Anthem or Solo — "The Words on the Cross," Part IV
Jesus, whelmed in fears unknown,
With our evil left alone,
While no light from heaven is shown;
    Hear us, holy Jesus.

When we seem in vain to pray,
And our hope seems far away,
In the darkness be our stay:
    Hear us, holy Jesus.

Though no Father seem to hear,
Though no light our spirits cheer,
May we know that God is near:
    Hear us, holy Jesus.

Prayer
    Dear God, we're often afraid and lonely. It seems as though we pray in vain. Our hope seems far away. We know in our hearts that you are near, but sometimes we forget.
    Stay close by us, when we are anxious. Do not leave us, when we need you. Help us always to remember that you love us, and that you will never leave us. Amen.

Scripture — Matthew 26:36-46
    Then Jesus brought them to a garden grove, Gethsemane, and told them to sit down and wait while he went on ahead to pray. He took Peter with him and Zebedee's two sons, James and John, and began to be filled with anguish and despair.
    Then he told them, "My soul is crushed with horror and sadness to the point of death . . . stay here . . . stay awake with me."
    He went forward a little, and fell face downward on the ground, and prayed, "My Father! If it is possible, let this cup be taken away from me. But I want your will, not mine."

Then he returned to the three disciples and found them asleep. "Peter," he called, "couldn't you even stay awake with me one hour? Keep alert and pray. Otherwise temptation will overpower you. For the spirit indeed is willing, but how weak the body is!" Again he left them and prayed, "My Father! If this cup cannot go away until I drink it all, your will be done."

He returned to them again and found them sleeping, for their eyes were heavy, so he went back to prayer the third time, saying the same things again.

Reflections of Matthew

Hymn — "Jesus, I My Cross Have Taken"

Extinguishing of Fourth Candle — Silent meditation

* Quiet meditation, with soft music

Hymn — "Go to Dark Gethsemane"

Reflections of Peter

Scripture — Luke 22:54-62

So they seized him and led him to the High Priest's residence, and Peter followed at a distance. The soldiers lit a fire in the courtyard and sat around it for warmth, and Peter joined them there.

A servant girl noticed him in the firelight and began staring at him. Finally she spoke: "This man was with Jesus!"

Peter denied it. "Woman," he said, "I don't even know the man!"

After a while someone else looked at him and said, "You must be one of them!"

"No, sir, I am not!" Peter replied.

About an hour later someone else flatly stated, "I know this fellow is one of Jesus' disciples, for both are from Galilee."

But Peter said, "Man, I don't know what you are talking about." And as he said the words, a rooster crowed.

At that moment Jesus turned and looked at Peter. Then Peter remembered what he had said — "Before the rooster crows tomorrow morning, you will deny me three times." And Peter walked out of the courtyard, crying bitterly.

Anthem or Solo — "The Words on the Cross," Part V
Jesus, in thy thirst and pain,
While thy wounds thy life-blood drain,
Thirsting more our love to gain:
Hear us, holy Jesus.

Thirst for us in mercy still,
All thy holy work fulfill,
Satisfy the loving will
Hear us, holy Jesus.

May we thirst thy love to know;
Lead us in our sin and woe
Where the healing waters flow:
Hear us, holy Jesus.

Pastor: Jesus said, "I thirst."

Psalm 40:11-17 — Read antiphonally
Right Side: O Lord, don't hold back your tender mercies from me! My only hope is in your love and faithfulness.
Left Side: Otherwise, I perish, for problems far too big for me to solve are piled higher than my head. Meanwhile, my sins, too many to count, have all caught up with me and I am ashamed to look up. My heart quails within me.
Right side: Please, Lord, rescue me! Quick! Come and help me! Confuse them! Turn them around and send them sprawling — all these who are trying to destroy me. Disgrace these scoffers

with their utter failure!

Left side: **But may the joy of the Lord be given to everyone who loves him and his salvation. May they constantly exclaim, "How great God is!"**

Prayer

Dear God, we're often influenced by the temptations of this world. Help us to be true to the high standards you have set for us. Support us as we seek to love our enemies, as we try to forgive seventy times seven, and as we put our trust in your loving will. Amen.

Reflections of Philip

Hymn — "There Is a Fountain Filled with Blood"

Extinguishing of Fifth Candle — Silent meditation

* Quiet meditation, with soft music

Hymn — "Glory Be to Jesus"

Reflections of Simon

Psalm 22:12-21 — Read responsively

I am surrounded by fearsome enemies, strong as the giant bulls from Bashan.

They come at me with open jaws, like roaring lions attacking their prey.

My strength has drained away like water, and all my bones are out of joint.

My heart melts like wax; my strength has dried up like sun baked clay; my tongue sticks to my mouth, for you have laid me in the dust of death.

The enemy, this gang of evil men, circles me like a pack of dogs; they have pierced my hands and feet.

I can count every bone in my body. See these

men of evil gloat and stare; they divide my clothes among themselves by a toss of the dice. O Lord, don't stay away. O God, my Strength, hurry to my aid. Rescue me from death; spare my precious life from all these evil men.

Save me from these lions' jaws and from the horns of these wild oxen. Yes, God will answer me and rescue me.

Pastor: Jesus said, "It is finished."

Anthem or Solo — "The Words on the Cross," Part VI
Jesus, all our ransom paid,
All thy father's will obeyed:
By thy sufferings perfect made:
    Hear us, holy Jesus.

Save us in our soul's distress;
Be our help to cheer and bless,
While we grow in holiness:
    Hear us, holy Jesus.

Brighten all our heavenward way
With an ever holier ray
Till we pass to perfect day;
    Hear us, holy Jesus.

Scripture — Revelation 5:6-10
I looked and saw a Lamb standing there before the twenty-four Elders, in front of the throne and the Living Beings, and on the Lamb were wounds that once had caused his death. He had seven horns and seven eyes, which represent the seven-fold Spirit of God, sent out into every part of the world. He stepped forward and took the scroll from the right hand of the one sitting upon the throne. And as he took the scroll, the twenty-four Elders fell down before the Lamb, each with a harp and golden vials filled with incense — the prayers of God's people! They were singing him a new song with these

words: "You are worthy to take the scroll and break its seals and open it; you were slain, and your blood has brought people from every nation as gifts for God. And you have gathered them into a kingdom and made them priests of our God; they shall reign upon the earth."

Prayer

Almighty God, we praise you and we thank you, for sending your only Son to die on the Cross for us. May our hearts be so firm with steadfast faith in him that we may not fear the power of evil in our lives. Help us to remember our Lord's suffering and death that we may obtain forgiveness for all our sins. Amen.

Hymn — "O Come and Mourn"

Extinguishing of Sixth Candle — Silent meditation

* Quiet meditation, with soft music

Hymn — "O Perfect Life of Love"

Reflections of Thomas

Psalm 130 — **Read in unison**

O Lord, from the depths of despair I cry for your help: "Hear me! Answer! Help me!"
Lord, if you keep in mind our sins, then who can ever get an answer to his prayers? But you forgive! What an awesome thing this is! That is why I wait expectantly, trusting God to help, for he has promised. I long for him more than sentinels long for the dawn.
O Israel, hope in the Lord; for he is loving and kind, anc comes to us with armloads of salvation. He himself shall ransom Israel from her slavery to sin.

Pastor: Jesus said, "Father, into thy hands I commend

my spirit."

Anthem or Solo — "The Words on the Cross," Part VII
Jesus, all thy labor past,
All thy woe and conflict past;
Yielding up thy soul at last;
    Hear us, holy Jesus.

When the death shades round us lower,
Guard us from the tempter's power,
Keep us in that trial hour:
    Hear us, holy Jesus.

May thy life and death supply
Grace to live and grace to die,
Grace to reach the home on high:
    Hear us, holy Jesus. Amen.

Scripture — Luke 23:44-46

By now it was noon, and darkness fell across the whole land for three hours, until three o'clock. The light from the sun was gone — and suddenly the thick veil hanging in the temple split apart. Then Jesus shouted, "Father, I commit my spirit to you," and with those words he died.

Litany

Pastor: Dear Jesus, you have died that we might live.

People: Humbly, we thank you.

Pastor: You have suffered that we might be forgiven.

People: Humbly, we thank you.

Pastor: You will rise again that we might have eternal life.

People: Humbly, we thank you.

Pastor: Make us strong in our faith and secure in our hope that we may die to rise again with you.

People: Humbly, we ask you. Amen.

Hymn — "Just as I Am"

Extinguishing of Seventh Candle — Silent meditation

Benediction

In our grief we go forth now, to meditate, to witness and to serve. In the name of the Father, and of the Son, and of the Holy Spirit. Amen.

(The congregation is asked to leave the church in silence.)